# SQUARES

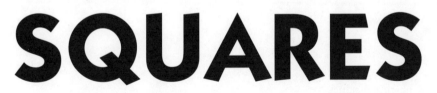

## Shapes in Math, Science and Nature

Written by Catherine Sheldrick Ross
Illustrated by Bill Slavin

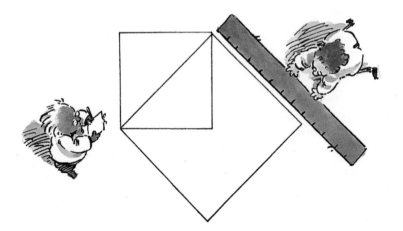

Kids Can Press Ltd.
Toronto

Kids Can Press Ltd. acknowledges with appreciation the assistance of the Canada Council and the Ontario Arts Council in the production of this book.

**Canadian Cataloguing in Publication Data**

Ross, Catherine Sheldrick
    Squares

(Shapes in math, science and nature)
Includes index.
ISBN 1-55074-273-6

1. Square — Juvenile literature.  I. Slavin, Bill.
II. Title.  III. Series: Ross, Catherine Sheldrick.
Shapes in math, science and nature.

QA482.R677   1996   j516'.15   C95-932357-0

Many of the designations used by manufacturers and sellers to distinguish their products are claimed as trademarks. Where those designations appear in this book and Kids Can Press Ltd. was aware of a trademark claim, the designations have been printed in initial capital letters (e.g., Lego).

Neither the Publisher nor the Author shall be liable for any damage which may be caused or sustained as a result of conducting any of the activities in this book without specifically following instructions, conducting the activities without proper supervision, or ignoring the cautions contained in the book.

Kids Can Press Ltd.
29 Birch Avenue
Toronto, Ontario, Canada
M4V 1E2

Edited by Laurie Wark
Designed by Esperança Melo

Printed and bound in Hong Kong

96  0 9 8 7 6 5 4 3 2 1

# Contents

# Acknowledgements

To start with, thanks to the academic and public libraries that made available hundreds of essential books, especially these: Thomas F. Banchoff, *Beyond the Third Dimension* (1990); Keith Critchlow, *Order in Space* (1969); H. Martyn Cundy and A.P. Rollett, *Mathematical Models* (1961); Alan Holden, *Shapes, Space and Symmetry* (1971); Spiro Kostoff, *The City Shaped* (1991); Peter Pearce, *Structure in Nature is a Strategy for Design* (1978); Marjorie Senechal and George Fleck, eds. *Shaping Space: A Polyhedral Approach* (1988); and Peter S. Stevens, *Patterns in Nature* (1974).

The production of a book is always a team effort. In the making of *Squares*, Professor Douglas Edge of the Faculty of Education, University of Western Ontario, provided invaluable help by reading the manuscript, making suggestions, and clarifying some tricky mathematical points. David Hamilton and First Folio made both substantive and copy-editing suggestions that were immensely helpful. And an especial thanks, as always, to the team at Kids Can Press who were co-creators of this whole series — Laurie Wark who provided the inspired editing; Esperança Melo who combined type and illustration into integrated spreads; and Bill Slavin whose genius at illustration has brought the text to life.

# Introduction

If you stand with your arms stretched out, you're about as tall and as wide as a square. A square is a shape with four equal sides and four equal angles. Look around and you'll see lots of square shapes — checkerboards, computer disks, waffles, floor tiles and square window panes. The rooms of your home are probably either squares or rectangles. You may live on a street that's part of a square city block. Even in rock paintings and in the earliest writing systems, the square was used as a symbol for the house or settlement.

People used to believe that the square was lucky and had magical powers. In the middle ages, Europeans would wear a silver disc with a square cut into it on a necklace to protect them from the Black Death plague.

Squares are flat. But if you put six squares together in the right way, you get a cube. You can find cubes in nature as crystals, such as the salt crystals you put on your vegetables. Architects like cubes for building because cubes can fit together side-by-side or they can stack, like blocks, into high-rise towers.

When you read *Squares*, you'll discover why cities are laid out in square blocks, solve some brain-teasers, find out about buildings that architects make from squares and cubes, navigate your way through square mazes, experiment with prisms and antiprisms, blow cube-shaped bubbles and much more.

If you find a square word you don't understand, check the glossary on page 62 for an explanation.

# 1 Amazing Squares

The number four is the most important thing about the square. Every square has four sides of equal length. And every square has four equal angles. Do the square test on this book — it looks sort of square, with four sides and four equal angles. To know for sure if it's a square, you'll have to measure to see if the four sides are exactly the same length.

## THE SQUARE UP CLOSE

A **right angle** is an angle of 90°. A square has four right angles.

**90°**

A **vertex** is a point where two sides meet. A square has four vertices.

The **midpoint** is the point that divides a side into two equal parts.

A **diagonal** is a straight line joining two opposite vertices of a square. A square has two diagonals.

The opposite sides of a square are **parallel**, which means that they're always the same distance apart.

# What is a square?

Mathematicians use lots of fancy terms to describe a square. A square is a **quadrilateral** — which means it's a polygon, or closed shape, with four sides. A square is also a **rectangle** — a quadrilateral with 4 right angles. A square is a **parallelogram** — a quadrilateral with opposite sides that are parallel. And finally a square is a **rhombus**, which is a parallelogram with four sides the same length.

CLOSED SHAPE WITH FOUR SIDES? ✓

FOUR RIGHT ANGLES? ✓

OPPOSITE SIDES PARALLEL? ✓

FOUR SIDES THE SAME LENGTH? ✓

You can figure out how far it is around the outside of a square (its perimeter) by multiplying the length of one side by 4.

# Making squares

Since the days of the cave-dwellers, people have been making squares — drawing them on cave walls, carving them into stone and using them to decorate temple walls. You can draw a square free-hand. But if you want a perfect square, here are two methods that work every time.

## Folding a square

**You'll need:**

a rectangular piece of paper, such as typing paper or a sheet of newspaper
scissors

1. Fold a short side of the paper so that it exactly touches a long side to make a triangle.

2. Fold the remaining paper over the triangle. Crease the fold line with your thumb.

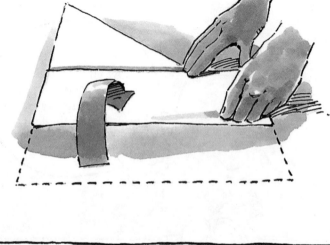

3. Unfold the paper and cut off the extra piece along the creased fold line.

4. You now have a square. The fold line dividing the square into two equal triangles is a diagonal of the square.

# Drawing a square

**You'll need:**
a piece of paper
a pencil
a ruler
a compass

1. Use a pencil and ruler to draw a straight line at least 5 cm (2 inches) from the bottom edge of the paper. Mark each end of this line with a dot and label this line AB. This line will be the lower side of your square.

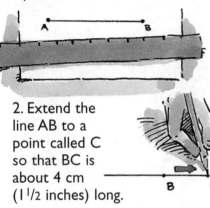

2. Extend the line AB to a point called C so that BC is about 4 cm (1½ inches) long.

3. Set the compass opening to the same distance as BC. Put the compass foot on point B. Draw an arc to intersect AB at D.

4. Make the compass opening a bit larger and put the compass foot on point D. Draw two arcs above and below the line.

5. Without changing the compass opening, put the compass foot on point C. Draw a second pair of arcs above and below the line to cut, or intersect, the first arcs.

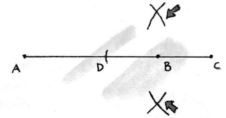

6. Use your ruler to draw a line through the two points where the arcs intersect, or meet. Extend the line toward the top of the paper. You have just made a 90° angle here — the first corner of your square.

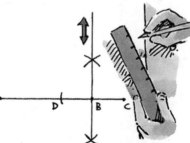

7. Set the compass opening to AB (remember that's the length of the side). Put the compass foot on point B and draw an arc above the base line to cut the vertical, or up-and-down, line at E.

8. Without changing the compass opening, set the compass foot on E and draw an arc.

9. In the same way, set the compass foot on A and draw a second arc, intersecting the first arc at F.

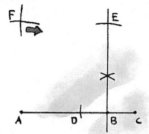

10. Use your ruler to draw lines to join AF and FE. Your square is AFEB.

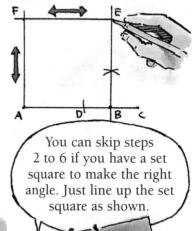

You can skip steps 2 to 6 if you have a set square to make the right angle. Just line up the set square as shown.

# Area of a square

If you ever have to carpet the floor of a square tree-house, here's how you can tell how much carpet to buy. You have to be able to figure out the area of the square, but luckily that's easy. All you do is multiply the length of one side of the square by itself. So if the square floor has a side that's 3 m (10 feet) long, then the area of the square is 3 times 3, or 9 square metres (100 square feet).

Now that you've mastered the basics of working out the area of a square, here are some fancy tricks you can do with areas.

**Doubling the square**
Draw a diagonal line through a square. Use this diagonal as the side for a second square. This second square is always twice as big as the original square. This means that the area of the square drawn on the diagonal is two times the area of the original square.

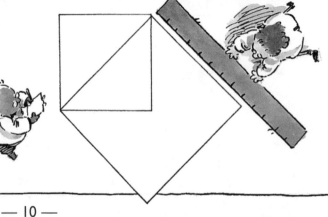

# Square multiplication

Here's a way to multiply the size of a square to double, triple, or quadruple it, or even make it ten times as big as the original square.

**You'll need:**
paper
a pencil
a ruler
a compass

1. Start with a small square ABCD drawn in the bottom corner of a piece of paper.

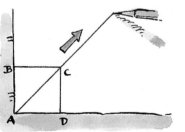

2. Draw the diagonal of the square AC and extend the line.

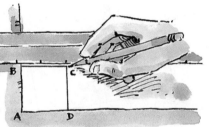

3. Extend the line BC right across the paper to form the line BE.

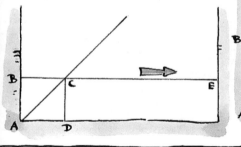

4. Put the compass foot on A and the pencil on C. Draw an arc to touch the bottom of the paper at F. The line AF is the side of a second square that's twice as big as your original square. Draw this square.

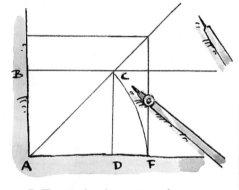

5. To triple the original square, put the the compass foot on A and the pencil on the point where BE cuts the right side of the second square. Draw an arc. The point where the arc touches the bottom of the paper is the bottom right-hand corner of the third square.

6. There are two secrets to drawing all the next squares. First, always keep the compass foot on A. Second, put the pencil on the point where BE cuts the right side of the previous square and draw an arc to touch the bottom of the paper. Eventually you'll go right off the paper.

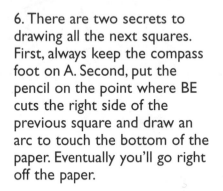

# Squaring off

Can you turn five small, equal-sized squares into one large, perfect square? The big square will, of course, have to be five times the size of the small square. Check it out for yourself.

**You'll need:**
a piece of paper
a ruler
a compass
a pencil
scissors

1. Draw five identical squares in a row with sides of 3 cm (1 inch).

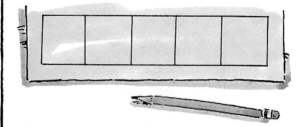

2. Cut out the row of five squares.

3. Cut off two squares. Draw a diagonal line through the two squares as shown and cut along the diagonal line.

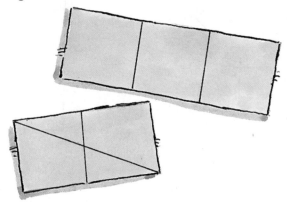

4. Repeat step 3 with a second set of squares.

5. Use the five pieces to make a single, perfect square. (See page 60 for the answer.)

# FOUR SQUARE

Squares are associated with lots of things that come in fours. Very old maps show Earth as a flat square, with the four winds coming from the four compass points of north, south, east and west. In some mythologies, four pillars on a square base hold up the whole world. Ancient legends often describe Earth as a square, with a giant or angel at each corner. In a Yucatan Indian myth, four ancestors at each corner of the square world hold up the heavens.

# SQUARE TALK

Real square

Back to square one

A square meal

A square deal

Winning fair and square

A square peg in a round hole

Squaring accounts

# Square numbers

You can use a handful of pebbles or pennies to unlock the secrets of square numbers — the same way Pythagoras did 2500 years ago. Pythagoras was a Greek mathematician who studied numbers by arranging pebbles into different geometric shapes. Arrange your pebbles into square shapes like these.

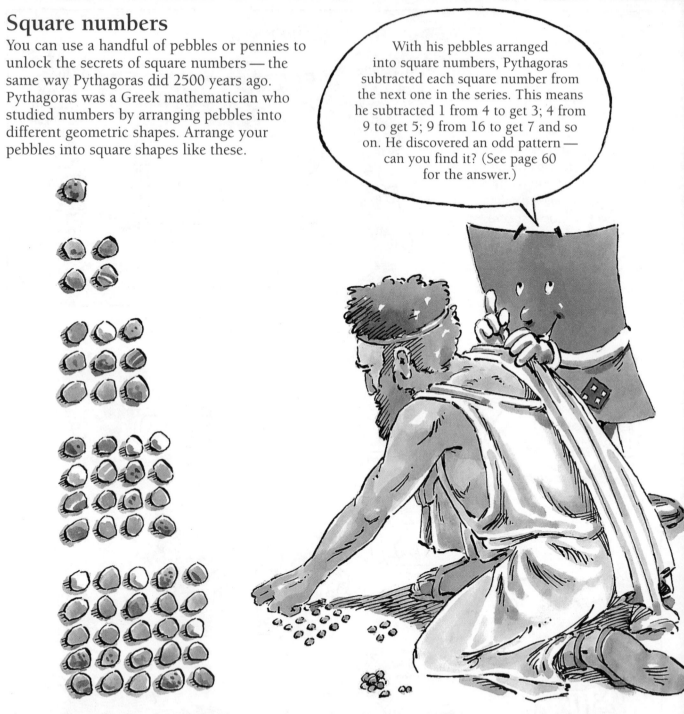

With his pebbles arranged into square numbers, Pythagoras subtracted each square number from the next one in the series. This means he subtracted 1 from 4 to get 3; 4 from 9 to get 5; 9 from 16 to get 7 and so on. He discovered an odd pattern — can you find it? (See page 60 for the answer.)

If you add up the number of pebbles in each square arrangement, you get the first five square numbers: 1, 4, 9, 16, 25. What are the next five square numbers? It's easy to figure out once you spot the pattern. To get the square number, you square the number, or multiply it by itself: $1 \times 1 = 1$; $2 \times 2 = 4$; $3 \times 3 = 9$; $4 \times 4 = 16$ and so on to $9 \times 9 = 81$ and $10 \times 10 = 100$. So the first ten square numbers are: 1, 4, 9, 16, 25, 36, 49, 64, 81, 100.

# A square story

According to an old story, the Shah of Persia was very impressed with a new game called chess that had just been invented. So he summoned the inventor to give him a reward. "Name it and it's yours," said the Shah. All the inventor asked for was some wheat. "Give me one grain of wheat on the first square of the chess board, twice as much on the second square, twice as much again on the third square, and so on, doubling each time, to the 64th square." "Only some wheat? But you can ask for anything — how about some silver plates or golden goblets? Wouldn't you like a herd of fine camels?" But the inventor said he was a simple man and wanted only wheat.

Imagine the Shah's surprise and annoyance when he discovered that it would take more wheat than he had in his whole kingdom to keep his promise. The number of grains of wheat mounts up fast when you keep doubling. On the eighth square there are 128 grains of wheat; on the ninth square, there are 256 grains; on the tenth square, there are 512 grains; and on the 31st square, there are over a billion grains of wheat.

# Square illusions

## Hermann grid

The Hermann grid is a tricky optical illusion of black square blocks separated by white lines, or streets. Hold this illustration at arm's length and look at the black blocks. At the intersections of the white streets, can you see a faint grey dot? The grey dot is an optical illusion caused by the contrast of black and white. The white looks whiter when it's surrounded by black. The white in the streets has more contrasting black around it than the white in the intersections. Check this out. Cover up the black blocks so that you can see only one street. What happens to the grey dots?

## Target practice

Is this a square or not? Check the sides against a ruler to find out.

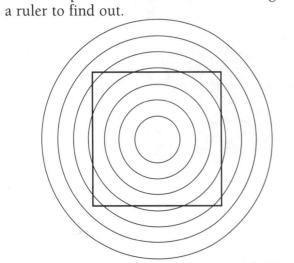

## Which is bigger?

1. If this were a square cake, which piece would you rather have if you were very hungry — the square piece inside or the amount that's left over when you take the square piece away?

2. Which diagonal is longer — the diagonal of the square or the diagonal of this Cretan double axe?

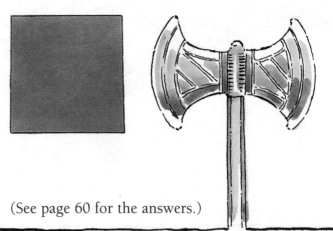

(See page 60 for the answers.)

## Jacob's ladder

Decorate your Christmas tree the way the early pioneers did, with homemade ornaments. This accordion shape, called a Jacob's ladder, is an easy decoration to make. Fold two paper strips into interlocking squares, put a thread through it and hang it up.

**You'll need:**
2 contrasting colours of construction paper
scissors
white glue

1. From one piece of construction paper, cut four or five strips about 3 cm (1 inch) wide. Glue together enough strips to make one piece about 1 m (3 feet) long.

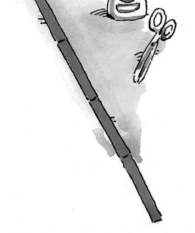

2. Repeat step 1, using a contrasting colour of construction paper.

3. Put some glue on one end of one of the strips. Place this gluey end on top of one end of the other strip, so that the strips form a right angle.

4. Fold the bottom strip over the top strip.

5. Repeat this step, folding the bottom strip over the top strip, until you run out of paper. You should end up with interlocking squares, folded on top of each other like an accordion.

6. Trim off any extra paper and glue the last two squares together.

# Square puzzlers

You'll need to put your thinking cap on before starting this foursome of square puzzles. (See page 60 for the answers.)

## How many squares?

To make this brain-teaser, start with a square piece of paper.

1. Fold the square of paper in half and sharpen the fold line between your thumb and first finger. Open the paper.

2. Repeat step 1, folding the square of paper in half in the other direction.

3. Fold each side to touch the midline and sharpen the fold line. Open the paper each time before folding the next side. You now have a square of paper folded into 16 small squares.

4. Count the squares. How many different squares can you find altogether? (Don't say 16.)

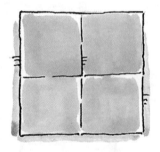

# What's my shape?

This puzzle is a shape-changer — from square, to cross, to loops, to what?

## You'll need:

a square piece of paper (any size will do, but a very small square of paper is convenient)

scissors

sticky tape

1. Fold the square piece of paper in half.

2. Fold it in half again in the other direction to make a smaller square.

3. Cut out a small square on the sides away from the fold lines.

4. Unfold the paper, which will now be in the shape of a cross.

5. Tape the ends of the cross together to form two loops at right angles to each other.

6. The final step is to cut along the original fold lines. Can you guess what shape you'll get? Get out your scissors to find out.

## Square dissection puzzle

Can you turn a square into a triangle? (See page 60 for the answer.)

**You'll need:**
a piece of thick paper or
    cardboard
a compass
a ruler
a pencil
scissors

1. Following the instructions on page 9, make a square with sides 10 cm (4 inches) long.

2. Mark the midpoint of each side.

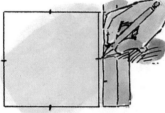

3. Connect the midpoints of two adjacent, or touching, sides.

4. Mark the place where a diagonal cuts the line you made in step 3 and call this point P.

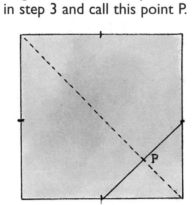

5. Draw lines from P to the midpoints of the opposite sides.

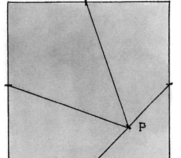

6. Cut along the three lines so that you end up with four pieces.

7. Reassemble these four pieces to make a triangle.

Why are squares so hard to find?

Because they're never a-round.

## Square takeaway

These 24 toothpicks are arranged into a large square with nine smaller squares inside. Can you remove six toothpicks so that there are only two squares left inside? (See page 60 for the answer.)

## THE MAGIC SQUARE

Add up the numbers in any row, column or diagonal of this square. Whether you add across, up-and-down or slantwise, the answer is always the same. That's what makes it a magic square.

Magic squares were discovered by the Chinese over 2000 years ago and have fascinated people ever since. According to a Chinese legend, the Emperor Yu was walking beside the Yellow River when he saw a turtle with strange markings on its shell. He noticed that the shell was divided into squares and each square contained a different number of dots. When he counted up the dots, he got the same number — 15 — whether he added down a column, across a row or along a diagonal. The arrangement of numbers on the turtle's back became famous as a magic square, called Lo-Shu in China.

# 2 Living in squares

Imagine that you're a city planner about to design a new city. You'll need to draw a city plan, including streets and buildings. Don't forget to add some open spaces for parks. Chances are you'll draw square blocks and add some square buildings. Your city plan might look a bit like this one, painted on a wall in Turkey around 8500 years ago. The square houses are laid out in straight lines.

Unlike birds who hollow out nests into round shapes and beavers who build domed houses, human beings usually live in spaces that are shaped into squares. Read on to find out why the square has given its shape to many famous buildings and cities since ancient times.

# Grids

Guess which cities are easier to find your way around — cities laid out in square blocks or cities where a tangle of streets grew up from old cow paths? The city built on the square grid design, of course. Why? First, because grids are so simple — at every intersection, two straight lines cross each other without bending. And second, the squares formed by the intersecting lines are all identical. So every block is the same size and it's the same distance from one intersection to the next. Look at a map for the place where you live, and you'll probably see lots of squares.

# Grid art

Do you have a picture that you want to make bigger? No problem, if you use a square grid. On your original picture, draw a grid of squares as shown. Then decide how much bigger you want the copy to be. To make it twice as high and twice as wide, draw a grid of squares with a side twice the length of the original square. Then copy the picture, square by square.

You can stretch the picture lengthwise, if you make a grid from rectangles 2 units high and 1 unit wide.

And you can distort the picture in weird ways, if you do this.

You can stre-e-e-tch the picture sideways, if you make a grid from rectangles 1 unit high and 2 units wide.

# Square cities

This 4500-year-old ceramic pattern from India shows two ancient town plans. Both are based on the square and the number four. Since then, the square has been nearly everybody's favourite shape for town planning.

4500-year-old
town plans
from India

Rome was called a squared city. When the Romans extended their empire into Europe and beyond, they brought their square plans with them. They reshaped the existing settlements into squares and they built new square settlements according to standard plans. The most basic plan was the *castrum* or military camp. It was designed on a grid plan with a small square at the centre where troops assembled.

Roman military camp

Here's one layout for a square city that fortunately was never built. In 1619, a philosopher, Johan Andreae, developed this maze-like plan for an ideal city, called Christianopolis. If you were in the outside square, how would you get to the centre?

Johan Andreae's plan for an ideal city

Circleville, Ohio, started off in 1810 as a circular city. But the square won out, little by little. By 1856, nothing remained of the circle that gave the town its name.

1837

1838

Circleville, Ohio, 1810

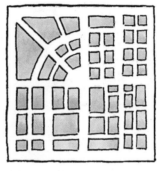
1849

1856

## SURVEYING

The lines we see in nature are all curves. Look at the outlines of coastlines, riverbeds, ponds, forests and mountain ranges and you won't see a single right angle or straight line. But when the Spanish, French and English settlers came to the forests of North and South America, they brought the right angle with them. They mapped out, or surveyed, the landscape into squares. This map shows one of the first townships surveyed in Ohio, U.S., around 1785. Surveyors were told to lay out square townships and one-square-mile farms. But as you can see, the surveyors can't make the river follow a straight line.

# City squares

Is there a town square or city square where you live? Squares are great places for people to get together. Sometimes city squares have developed all by themselves at the crossing of two important roads. And sometimes city planners designed a square for the town centre right from the beginning.

Lots of squares are just as famous as the cities they're in — there's St. Peter's Square in Rome, St. Mark's Square in Venice and Red Square in Moscow. Some squares aren't even square, actually being longer than they are wide! Here are some remarkable city squares.

**Aztec capital at Tenochtitlan (Mexico City)**
In 1519, when Hernan Cortés and his Spanish soldiers reached the Aztec capital, they found a city twice the size of the largest city in Spain. At the centre of this city was a ceremonial plaza made of polished stone. This plan, probably drawn by Cortés, shows a central square on an island surrounded by water and connected to the mainland by causeways. Within three years, Cortés completely destroyed the city.

**Grenade-sur-Garonne in France**
Mathematicians must have planned this market square. The market block at the centre of this French town is a perfect square. But each block to the east or west of the centre block gets progressively bigger. The secret to the distance between the blocks is that the length of each block is the diagonal of the smaller one beside it.

**Tiananmen Square in Beijing**
China had no tradition of public squares. But in 1949 the Communist leader Mao Zedong built a square in Beijing about the size of 90 football fields — so huge that a crowd of a million loyal farmers and workers could meet to wave flags and cheer his speeches. In 1989, Chinese students held a giant protest against the government in Tiananmen Square.

**Red Square in Moscow**
Russia's most famous gathering place is Red Square in Moscow, where the May Day parades are held each year. From Red Square, you can see the Great Kremlin Palace, which was built for the ruling Czars and now houses the Russian Parliament.

# Square buildings

Although most people were sold on square and rectangular buildings, the 19th-century American builder, Orson Squires Fowler, thought that the perfect form was the circle. Since circular houses are so hard to build, Fowler decided the next best thing was the octagonal building. Fowler built his own octagonal mansion at Fishkill, New York, and soon the fad for building Fowler octagons spread across North America. In the nineteenth century, people built octagonal houses, schools, churches and even octagonal barns. For most of human history, however, people have found the square a more practical shape for buildings. Check out some of these amazing square buildings from around the world.

## Le Corbusier's museum of unlimited extendability

Seen from above, this museum looks like a maze. The inner walls were made from same-sized units that could be put together in different ways. This meant that the walls could be moved around and changed to make inside spaces that would suit the exhibits.

## Santa Sophia

The Emperor Justinian completed the great church, Santa Sophia, in Constantinople (now Istanbul) in the year A.D. 537. It has a square central space inside that's covered by the great circular dome above.

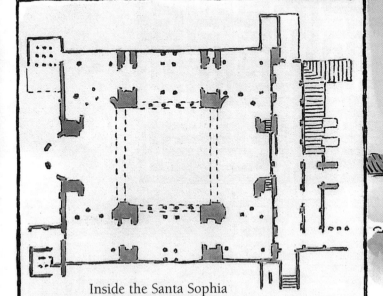

Inside the Santa Sophia

## Japanese houses

For more than a thousand years, the Japanese have used tatami to cover the floors of their houses. What's a tatami? It's a thick piece of matting that is the shape of two squares, set side by side. A single tatami is the right size to sleep on, about 2 m (6 feet) long and 1 m (3 feet) wide. When the Japanese design their houses, they use the tatami as a measuring unit. There are 4-tatami rooms, 4 1/2-tatami rooms, 8-tatami rooms, 10-tatami rooms and so on.

A 4 1/2-tatami room

# Square mazes

Mazes are tricky spaces that are easy to get lost in. Can you find the path to the centre of these square mazes? Turn to page 60 for the solutions.

### Church maze

This pavement maze in the abbey of St. Bertin at Saint-Omer in France was destroyed in the 18th century because it was too much fun. The noise of people running through the maze distracted attention from the church services.

### Garden maze

This design for a garden maze by G. A. Boeckler was published in 1664. It is a true puzzle maze: unlike the St. Bertin maze, it has branching paths and dead ends.

# THE GOLDEN RECTANGLE

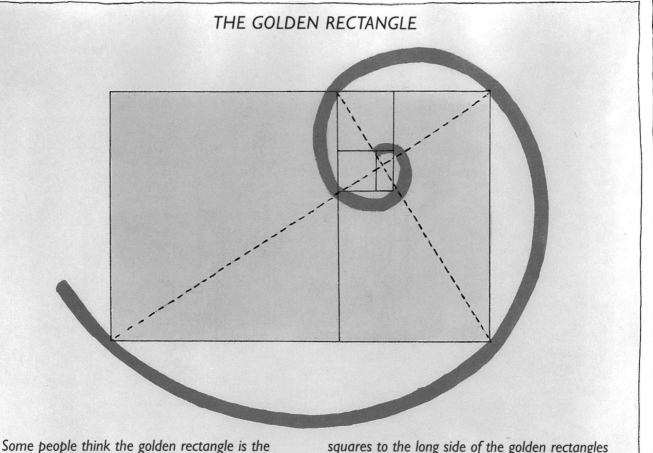

Some people think the golden rectangle is the most pleasing shape possible because they like its proportion of length to width. The ancient Greeks thought so and used the golden rectangle shape for building the Parthenon in Athens. Modern artists like the shape too and so most picture frames are golden rectangles.

To get a golden rectangle, you start with a square and find the midpoint of the base. Then you put the compass foot on this midpoint and the pencil on an opposite vertex. Draw an arc to intersect the line that extends from the base of the square. This intersection point is one corner of the golden rectangle.

It's easy to turn a golden rectangle into a spiral — you make more golden rectangles. To the first rectangle, attach a square with a side equal to the long side of the rectangle. Now you have a second, bigger golden rectangle. Continue attaching squares to the long side of the golden rectangles and you get a shape made of squares that spiral outward in ever-widening turns. This is the shape of regular growth in nature — when living things grow, their bodies become bigger but the parts keep the same proportions. So a snail shell gets bigger as it grows, but it always has the same shape.

# 3 Square designs

The square is about the simplest shape you can make, with its repetition of equal sides and right angles. But if you're making a design that uses squares, don't worry that all the good ideas have been used up. Thousands of different square designs are possible.

Take a look at some square designs from all over the world, from cave drawings to the most modern art. These designs have decorated walls, fabrics, quilts and canvas.

The cross was an ancient sign of great power long before it became a Christian symbol. This is a Jerusalem cross.

In this ancient Egyptian design, the square takes 90° or quarter turns.

The Mayas built great temples based on geometric forms. Squares decorate the walls of the Maya temple of Uxmal in Yucatan, Mexico.

The walls of the Alhambra, the Muslim palace in Granada, Spain, are covered with intricate, geometric patterns like this one.

The Dutch artist Piet Mondrian just couldn't stop painting squares. He gave his pictures names like "Place de la Concorde" and "Composition with red," but to most people the paintings look like squares and rectangles.

Quilt-makers in North America a hundred years ago created this illusion of tumbling cubic blocks by using a single diamond piece arranged into a hexagon. The secret is to use three shades of colour in the same position throughout the quilt — one light, one medium and one dark.

# Tumbling blocks

Make your own tumbling blocks pattern.

**You'll need:**
3 colours of Bristol board
a pencil
a compass
a ruler
scissors

1. Use the compass to draw a circle — 5 cm (2 inches) is a convenient compass opening to use. Without changing the compass opening, mark off six division points on the circle.

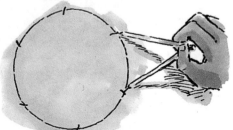

2. Use your ruler to draw lines to connect the division points. You have made a hexagon.

3. From the circle's centre, draw a line to every second division point to make three diamonds.

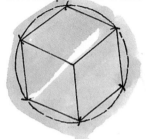

4. Cut out the diamonds.

5. Repeat steps 1 to 4 to make more diamonds. You'll need at least four diamond shapes in each colour of Bristol board to make this tumbling block pattern.

# Printing with squares

Here's a quick way to use your favourite square pattern for making wrapping paper.

## You'll need:

white paper
corrugated cardboard (the kind used for grocery cartons)
a pencil
a ruler
a set square
scissors
white glue
2 or 3 paint brushes
2 or 3 contrasting colours of tempera or poster paint
newsprint or other paper to print your design on

1. Draw a square on white paper — sides of 7 cm (3 inches) work well. Cut out the square.

2. Fold the square in half once and in half again to make a small square. Unfold.

3. Fold the square in half once along the diagonal and in half again to make a small triangle. Unfold.

4. Cut along the fold lines so that you get eight right-angled triangles. To design a printing pattern in which half the area of the original square is coloured, throw away four triangles and use the other four triangles to make a pattern.

5. Try arranging the triangles in different ways to decide on a pattern for your print. (There are 13 different patterns possible. After you've experimented to discover the pattern you like best, check page 61 to see if you've thought of all of them.)

6. On corrugated cardboard, draw two squares the same size as the original paper square. Cut them out.

7. On one cardboard square, trace the design you decided on in step 5. Cut out the pieces.

8. Paste the pieces onto the second cardboard square to make a stamp for your design. When you print the pattern, the raised parts will be coloured and the rest will stay white.

9. Use different brushes to apply two or three colours of paint to the raised parts only.

10. Press the stamp onto the paper you are making into wrapping paper.

11. Reapply paint. Stamp the paper again alongside the first impression. Continue, until you cover the whole paper with the design.

If you hold the stamp the same way up each time, you get a design like the one in step 11— called a **translation** or a **slide**. For variety, **turn**, or rotate, the stamp to get a design like this.

## SAND DESIGNS

These designs in sand aren't made by artists but by vibrations of high-pitched sound. To make these designs, called Chladni figures, a physicist puts a little sand on a glass or metal plate. Then she places two fingers on the plate and, at the same time, draws a bow, like a violin bow, along the edge of the plate. The bow makes the plate vibrate, and the vibration causes the sand to shake itself into a pattern. As you can see, square plates produce square-looking sand designs with 90° angles.

# Jeu de parquet

People in France used to play the game of parquet on a small table, using **64** porcelain square tiles of two colours. With this set of **16** squares, you'll still be able to make millions of different patterns with no repetitions.

## You'll need:

a square box, such as a chocolate box
black Bristol board
plain white paper
stiff cardboard, such as the backing of a notepad
a ruler
a pencil
scissors
a pin
glue

1. Take the top off the square box and set the top aside. Measure the length of the side of the bottom part of the box.

2. Subtract 0.5 cm (¹/4 inch) from this length. Draw a square on a piece of black Bristol board, using this shorter measurement as the length of the side. Cut out the square.

3. Cut out a square from white paper to be the same size as the black square.

4. Fold the white square into 16 small squares (see "How many squares?" on page 18). Sharpen each crease between your thumb and forefinger.

5. Place the white square over the black square so that it exactly matches.

— 36 —

6. Use a pin to poke a hole on the fold line, close to one edge of the square. Make sure that the pin goes through the two layers. Repeat this step so that you make a pinhole in three places along each side, on the foldlines.

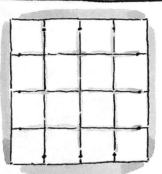

7. Set aside the white square until step 9. Use a ruler and pencil to draw lines on the black square to connect the pinholes. You should now have a grid of 16 squares.

8. Paste the large black square onto a stiff piece of cardboard. Cut out the 16 black squares.

9. Cut out 8 of the small squares from the folded square of white paper. Then cut each white square in half along the diagonal to form 2 triangles — 16 triangles in all.

10. Paste one white triangle on each black square to make a design unit.

11. Put the 16 design units into the square box. Start with the pieces all aligned the same way.

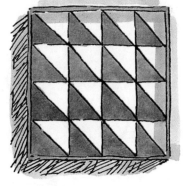

12. Now make your pattern. There are four possible positions for each square piece. Experiment by rotating the pieces until you produce a knock-out design.

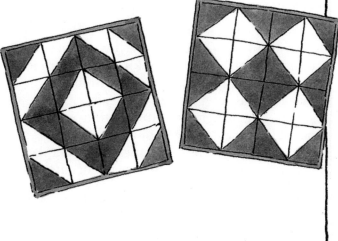

# Origami

Take a square and turn it into a bird, a fish, a box or a boat. You don't need to be a magician. You just need to know the craft of origami, which is the ancient Japanese art of paper-folding. Read the rules below, then make the origami crafts on the next pages.

**Basic rules of origami**

1. Work on a hard, flat, clean surface.

2. You'll need a square of paper — a square of 15 cm (6 inches) works well. If you don't have origami paper, many other kinds will work such as notepaper, gift paper or pages from a magazine, as long as the paper is cut into a square. The paper needs to be strong enough to be folded repeatedly without tearing or stretching. If you're using origami paper, place the coloured side face-down at the beginning.

3. Make every fold as straight as you can. Then run your thumbnail over the fold to make a sharp crease.

# Fortune teller

1. Fold a square of paper in half diagonally. Unfold. Fold the paper in half diagonally the other way. Unfold.

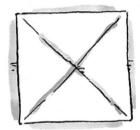

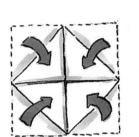

2. Fold all four corners in to touch the centre, where the diagonal folds cross each other.

3. Turn the paper over. Fold all corners to touch the centre.

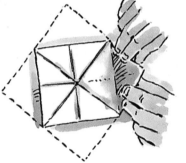

4. Fold the square in half so that the square flaps face out.

5. Fit your thumbs and forefingers into the compartments under the square flaps on each side and pinch. You can open and close this shape in two directions.

6. To add pizazz, colour the inside eight triangles in two contrasting shades such as red and green.

7. Turn your origami shape into a fortune teller by writing eight messages under the flaps — one message on each triangle. Next write the numbers from 1 to 8 on the top of the flaps.

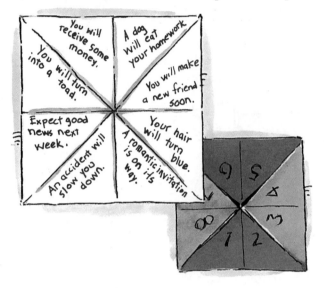

8. Now you're ready to tell a fortune. Get a friend to pick a number from 1 to 8. Open and close the fortune teller that many times. Now ask your friend to pick one of the exposed numbers on the flap. Read out the fortune under the chosen flap.

# Whale

1. Fold a square of paper in half diagonally from corner to corner. Unfold.

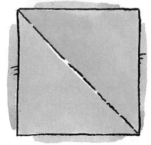

2. Fold one of the other corners in to touch the diagonal.

3. Repeat step 2 with the last corner.

4. Turn the shape over so that the flaps are underneath. Fold it in half along the diagonal line you made in step 1.

5. Fold the nose back along the diagonal fold line as shown. Crease and unfold. Push the nose inside the body by folding along the line you just made.

6. Fold the tail up. Crease and unfold.

7. Pick up the head of the whale in one hand, with your forefinger and thumb along the centre crease. With your other hand, push the centre crease along the tail inside the body. Fold along the crease line you made in step 6 to tuck the tail up and inside the body.

8. To make the flippers, fold the flaps back.

9. Cut part of the way down the centre crease of the tail. Fold down to make fins.

10. You can hang your whale from a lightweight stick to make a mobile.

# Tangram

This tangram puzzle comes from China, where it is called Chi-Chiao, meaning "The Seven Clever Pieces." After you've cut these seven clever pieces from a square, you can use them to make a face, camel, whale, house, cat, sailboat — in fact, hundreds of different shapes.

**You'll need:**
stiff cardboard or Bristol board
a pencil
a ruler
scissors

1. On the cardboard, draw a square. For the side of the square, choose a length that is a multiple of four — for example, 16 or 20 cm (8 inches).

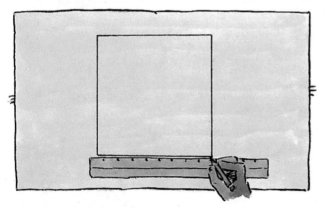

2. Using your ruler, make marks that divide the sides of the square into four equal segments. Draw faint lines to divide the large square into 16 small squares.

3. Draw lines as shown.

4. Cut out the seven pieces and you're ready to make these shapes or to invent your own.

Stumped on some of these shapes? Turn to page 61 for some answers.

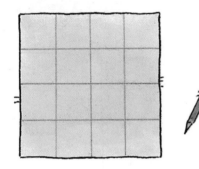

# Polyominoes

You likely know about dominoes, which are made from two identical squares connected along an edge. But how about trominoes (three squares), tetrominoes (four squares) or pentominoes, formed from five identical squares. An American puzzle mathematics professor, Solomon Golomb, invented the word "polyomino" to mean any set of identical squares connected along an edge.

Cut out four identical squares and use them to experiment with polyominoes. There is only one arrangement of squares to make a domino. There are only two ways to join three squares together to make a tromino — three squares in a row and an L shape. But there are five different tetrominoes — can you find them? (See page 61 for the answer.)

If a shape can be turned over to fit over another shape, the two shapes are considered mathematically the same.

## Pentominoes

With the 12 different pentominoes that can be made from 5 squares, you can make a game for two players.

**You'll need:**
paper
cardboard or Bristol board
a pencil
a ruler
scissors
glue

**To make the game pieces**
1. Cut a square out of paper — 16 cm (8 inches) makes a convenient size.

2. Carefully fold the square of paper exactly in half and sharpen the fold line between your thumb and first finger. Open the paper. Fold the square of paper in half in the other direction and sharpen the fold line. Open the paper.

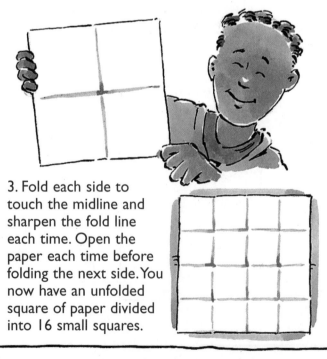

3. Fold each side to touch the midline and sharpen the fold line each time. Open the paper each time before folding the next side. You now have an unfolded square of paper divided into 16 small squares.

4. Fold the paper in half twice to make a smaller square. As in step 3, fold each side to touch the midline and sharpen the fold line each time. Unfold the paper.

5. Use your pencil and ruler to outline the four squares in the middle.

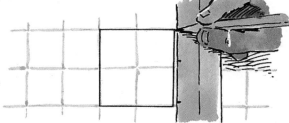

6. Follow the pattern shown here to outline all 12 pentominoes. Check that each shape you outline really is made from 5 squares.

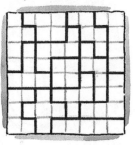

7. Paste the square of paper on a piece of cardboard or Bristol board. Cut out the square from the cardboard.

8. Trace the outline of this square onto another piece of cardboard. Cut out the second cardboard square and set it aside to use as your game board.

9. Cut up the first cardboard square into the 12 pentominoes. Throw away the square piece from the middle, which you outlined in step 5.

**To play the game**

1. Each player in turn picks a pentomino piece and places it on the board.

2. The object of the game is to prevent the other player from putting another piece on the board.

3. The player who makes the last move wins.

If you don't have a player to play against, use the pentomino pieces to solve these tricky puzzles. The bar is 3 squares wide and 20 squares long. The rectangle is 6 squares wide and 10 squares long. Each foot of the bridge is 3 squares wide. (See page 61 for answers.)

# 4 Cubes

If you roll a cube on a table, no matter how it lands it always looks the same. Unless you paint the faces different colours or mark them like dice, you can't tell which way is up or down and which way is front or back. Each cube has six same-sized square faces and, of course, they all meet at 90° angles.

This outline might look like a hopscotch pattern, but mathematicians call it a net and you can use it as a pattern to make a cube.

Check out cubic crystals for yourself. Examine a crystal of salt under a strong magnifying glass.

Architects like cubes because they fit together so well. Cubes pack together to fill space completely without leaving any air-holes in between. If oranges were cube-shaped instead of spherical, they would fill all the space in the orange crate and not just three-quarters of it.

Cubes happen in nature too. A fossil sponge is hollow but its supporting structure looks like the edges of a cube. Salt crystals are cubes and so is metallic iron. Both salt and iron are built up of very tiny building blocks that are cube-shaped. These building units are too small to see, but at the Brussels International Exhibit in 1958 the basic unit of iron was magnified 200 000 times to make a gigantic sculpture. To make the shape more dramatic, the sculptor tipped the cube onto one vertex.

# Cornered

Turn a flat piece of paper into a three-dimensional shape to find out the secrets of a cube's corners, or vertices.

**You'll need:**
paper
scissors
sticky tape

1. Fold a square piece of paper into quarters.

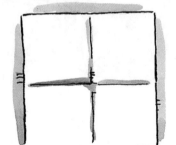

2. Cut a line from the midpoint of one side to the middle of the square.

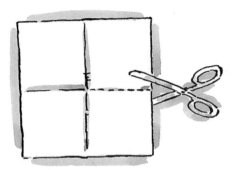

3. Now you are ready to experiment with shapes. Arrange three squares around a single point by overlapping the two squares that you cut apart in step 2. You get a closed corner, or vertex.

4. Arrange four squares around a single point and you have no corners, just a flat piece of paper.

5. How about five squares? If you cut out a fifth square the same size as the others, you can tape it into the cut opening. Now all five squares fit around a single point, but again you don't have a corner. You have a saddle shape that folds in and out.

**What's happening?**
As you can see, squares can fit together in only one way to enclose space and make a corner — you need three squares to fit around a single vertex. Six squares fit together to make a cube with six faces, eight corners or vertices and twelve edges.

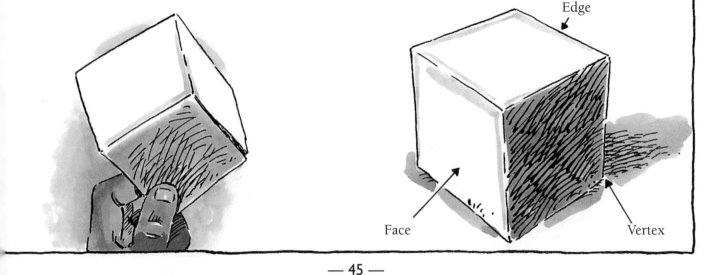

Edge

Face

Vertex

# Make a cube

Once you get the hang of making cubes, you can make them in different sizes from tiny to quite big. You can jazz up your cube with coloured markers for a gift box or write numbers on it to make a die. You can even print a pattern on your cube (see "Printing with squares" on page 34). Just remember that it's easier to decorate *before* you glue the faces together.

**You'll need:**
an index card
Bristol board or thick paper
a compass
a pencil
a ruler
scissors
white glue
coloured markers (optional)

1. In one corner of an index card, draw a square with 6-cm (2$\frac{1}{2}$-inch) sides. Cut out the square. You'll use this cardboard shape as a pattern to draw six squares on Bristol board or thick paper.

2. Place the cardboard square on the Bristol board and mark the four corners of the first square. Use a ruler to draw the lines.

3. Draw the other five squares the same way, in the pattern shown, to make a net.

4. Draw seven tabs as shown, about 0.5 cm ($\frac{1}{4}$ inch) wide.

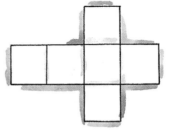

5. Lightly score the fold lines with the compass foot. This will make it easier to fold. But don't push too hard.

6. Cut out the net.

7. Crease the fold lines with your thumb. If you want to decorate the faces of your cube, now is the time to do it.

8. Put glue on the two tabs on one side-square, and attach to make a corner.

9. When this corner is dry, put glue on the two tabs on the other side-square and attach to make another corner.

10. When this corner is dry, put glue on the final three tabs and attach the last face of the cube.

> Make a bunch of boxes in graduated sizes and in different colours, and you have a nested set of gift boxes that fit inside each other. But don't glue the top flap down if you want to get the inside boxes out again.

## Dicey counting

This magic trick will amaze your friends, even math whizzes. It's based on the fact that each opposite pair of faces on a die adds up to 7.

**You'll need:**
three dice

1. Ask a friend to stack three dice in a column.

2. Turn your back while your friend adds up the numbers on the five hidden faces.

3. When your friend is ready, turn around, glance at the top face of the column of dice and quickly say, "Abracadabra, the answer is 17."

### How does it work?
The answer in this case is 17. Each opposite pair of faces on a die adds up to 7. So you know that the sum of the top and bottom faces on three dice is $3 \times 7$ or 21. You can see at a glance that the top face is 4. Therefore the hidden faces must be 21 minus 4, which is 17. If the top face were 6, the answer would be 21 minus 6 or 15.

# The Delian cube legend

In 430 B.C., a plague of typhoid fever swept over the Greek city of Athens. According to legend, the Athenians consulted the oracle at Delos for advice. The answer came back, "Apollo is angry. You must double the size of his altar here at Delos before the plague will end." The altar was in the shape of a cube. So the Athenians made a second cube identical to the first and set it alongside. This new altar was double in volume but, alas, it was no longer cube-shaped. This made Apollo more angry and he sent an even worse plague.

So the Athenians made a new cube, with edges twice as long as the edges of the original altar. Apollo got even angrier. What went wrong the second time? To find the volume of a cube, you multiply the length of the edge by itself three times. So if the original altar had a side that was 2 units long, its volume would be 2 times 2 times 2, which is 8 cubic units. When the Athenians doubled the length of the altar's side to 4 units, the volume of the new cube became 4 times 4 times 4, which is 64 cubic units — eight times as big. So instead of doubling the size, the Athenians had built a monster-altar, eight times the size of the original. Yikes! Check this out for yourself, using sugar cubes. If you use two sugar cubes for the length of a side, how many sugar cubes does it take altogether to make a cube?

The bad news for the Athenians is that the problem set by Apollo can't be solved. It's one of the mathematical impossibilities of the ancient world. It is impossible to double the cube if your only instruments are a compass and straight edge.

# Cubic puzzlers

If you don't find square puzzles challenging enough, here are some puzzles that add a whole extra dimension. (See page 61 for the answers to these cubic puzzlers.)

## Cube cuts

Suppose you have a 3-cm (3-inch) wooden cube. What is the smallest number of saw cuts you would have to make to get 27 cubes with 1-cm (1-inch) edges?

## Cross-sections of the cube

How would you slice a cube to get these shapes?

## Colouring a cube

Suppose you wanted to colour the faces of a cube so that each face is one solid colour and no adjacent, or touching, faces are the same colour. What is the smallest number of colours needed?

## Rotating a cube

If you take a flat penny and spin it around, you get the outline of a sphere. What shape do you get if you hold a cube on vertices along the long diagonal and spin it around?

a rectangle

a square

a hexagon

a triangle

Ask your parents if they remember the Rubik's Cube. In 1975, a Hungarian architect, Erno Rubik, invented this tricky cube made of 27 smaller cubes. Hungarian teachers used the Rubik's cube as a teaching aid in schools before it became a puzzle craze that swept the world.

# Cuboctahedron construction kit

With this construction kit, you can make cubes, cuboctahedra, square-based pyramids and other fancy shapes.

**You'll need:**

Bristol board or cardboard in
   at least two colours
a pencil
a ruler
a compass
scissors
a one-hole punch
a box of 5-cm (2-inch) elastics

1. On a piece of Bristol board or cardboard, draw a square with 10-cm (4-inch) sides. Use the compass foot to score the lines outlining the square.

2. Draw a slightly larger square as a 0.5-cm ($^1/_4$-inch) frame around the first one. Cut out the larger square.

3. Punch a hole at each corner of the small square. Trim the corners and fold up the edges along the score lines.

4. Make more square units the same way, using the same colour of Bristol board. You'll need 6 square units to make a cube.

5. Now make a triangular unit, using a different colour of Bristol board. Start by drawing a straight line 10 cm (4 inches) long. Put the compass foot on one end of the line and draw an arc as shown, keeping a compass opening of 10 cm (4 inches). Without changing the compass opening, put the compass foot on the other end of the line and draw a second arc to intersect the first one. Draw two lines to make the other two sides of the triangle.

6. Use the compass foot to score the lines outlining the triangle.

7. Draw a slightly larger triangle as a 0.5-cm ($^1/_4$-inch) frame around the first one. Cut out the larger triangle.

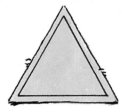

8. Punch a hole at each vertex of the small triangle. Trim the corners and fold up the edges along the score lines.

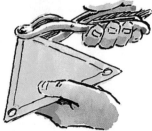

9. Make more triangular units the same way, using the same colour of Bristol board.

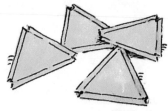

## Cube

1. Start by lining up two squares as shown. Join them by fitting an elastic over the punched holes.

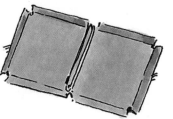

2. Use three more elastics and two more squares to make a four-sided column.

3. With four elastics, attach a square unit to form a top. Use another four elastics to attach the last square to complete the cube.

## Cuboctahedron

Jazz things up with a special shape called a cuboctahedron — it's like a cube with the corners sliced off. Use six squares of one colour and eight triangles of a contrasting colour.

1. Use an elastic to attach a triangle and a square together. Make a second triangle-square unit the same way.

2. Arrange these two triangle-square units around a single vertex so that the squares and triangles alternate. You've just made one vertex, or corner, of the cuboctahedron. In total, the cuboctahedron has twelve identical vertices, each one surrounded by two squares alternating with two triangles.

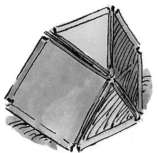

3. Use elastics to add more faces. Just make sure that you alternate squares and triangles so that the side of a triangle is always connected to the side of a square.

Here are some more neat shapes you can make with your construction kit.

Square-based pyramid
Use 1 square and
4 triangles.

Triangular prism
Use 3 squares
and 2 triangles.

Rhombicuboctahedron
Use 8 triangles, 6 squares
of one colour and 12
squares of a second colour.

# Prisms and antiprisms

When you think of prisms, you may think of a triangular piece of glass that breaks up the sunlight into rainbow colours. But the word prism really refers to a shape. A cube is a prism. A prism must have a base and a top that are parallel and the same size and shape, and the sides of a prism must be parallelograms. To identify a prism, count the sides in the prism's base — three sides make a triangular prism, four sides make a rectangular prism, five sides make a pentagonal prism and so on. The cube is a rectangular prism, in which all the faces are same-sized squares. Experiment with this cube made out of straws. Afterwards you can turn it into another neat shape called an antiprism.

**You'll need:**
a package of plastic straws
paper clips
pins

1. Start by making the connectors for the vertices of the cube. For each connector, join three paper clips. Make eight connectors.

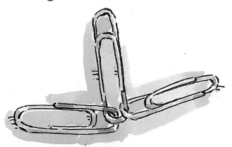

2. Fit two straws over the outside clips of one connector.

3. Fit an outside connector clip into the open end of these two straws.

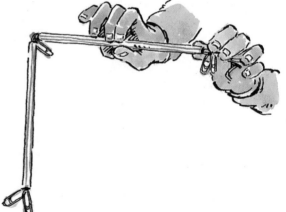

4. Make a square by fitting two more straws over the other outside clip on each connector.

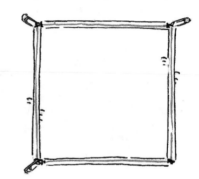

5. Use a fourth connector to attach the last corner of the square.

6. Fit a straw over each of the four middle clips.

7. Now finish the job by adding the other four connectors and four more straws.

8. Your cube is ready to stand up. Oops! What happened? Very likely your 12 connected straws fell flat on the table in an interesting pattern. Move it a bit and you get another interesting pattern, but not a cube.

9. What to do? Add a triangle, which is the only structure that can't be pushed out of shape. Use a straw and two pins, as shown, to make the triangle. Make sure that the triangle you make contains a 90° angle.

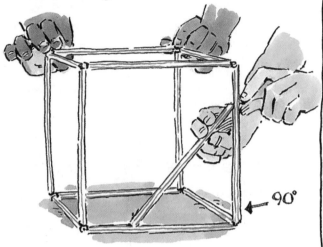

10. Keep adding straws to make triangles, as in step 9, until the cube is rigid and won't wobble out of shape. What is the least number of straws you need to make the cube stand up? Check page 61 to see if you're right.

## To make an antiprism

Now that you've made a square-based prism, you can turn it into a square antiprism. You discovered that the top and bottom faces must be lined up perfectly in a prism, one exactly above the other. In an antiprism, one of these faces is given a turn. Each vertex of the top face ends up directly above the midpoints of the sides of the bottom face.

1. Start with the straw cube you made on page 53. Keep the two triangles that brace the top and bottom faces but remove the four triangles that brace the sides.

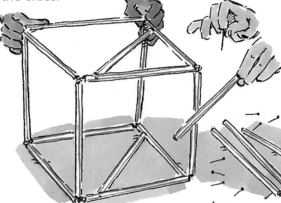

2. Add an extra paper clip to the eight connectors making the vertices of the cube.

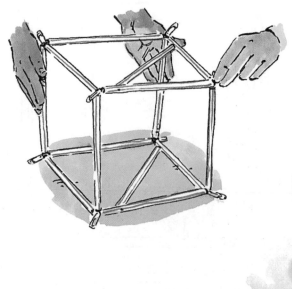

3. Fit four straws over the extra paper clips on the top face.

4. Attach the other ends of these four straws to the extra paper clips on the bottom face. There you have it — a square antiprism. As you see, this square antiprism has only two square faces. All the other faces are equilateral triangles.

Hmmm …
2 square faces
8 triangular faces

— 54 —

# IMPOSSIBLE CUBES

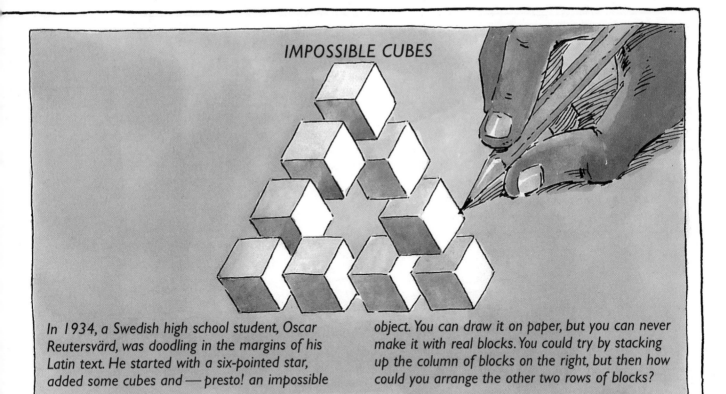

In 1934, a Swedish high school student, Oscar Reutersvärd, was doodling in the margins of his Latin text. He started with a six-pointed star, added some cubes and — presto! an impossible object. You can draw it on paper, but you can never make it with real blocks. You could try by stacking up the column of blocks on the right, but then how could you arrange the other two rows of blocks?

$$F + V = E + 2$$

What is this — a secret code? a recipe for ice cream? Actually it's Euler's formula, discovered by Leonhard Euler (pronounced oiler). This formula shows us the relationship between the number of faces, vertices and edges that works for every kind of polyhedron — yep, every single one. The number of faces (F) plus the number of vertices (V) equals the number of edges (E) plus 2. Check this out on the cube — 6 faces + 8 vertices = 12 edges + 2.

# Cubic architecture

Anyone who has ever played with blocks knows that cubes fit together perfectly to fill space. Most other solid shapes fit together leaving big gaps and air-holes in between. Cylindrical cans of soup waste space on the grocery-store shelf because of the spaces between the cans. But cartons in the shape of cubes or rectangular prisms pack together efficiently to use up all the room on the shelf. Architects like to pack cubes together too. And when they get bored stacking cubes into straight columns, they try some variations. Here are two unusual buildings made from cubes.

**Safdie's Habitat**

Moshe Safdie designed this housing project for Expo '67, the World's Fair in Montreal, Canada. Each of these apartments is a cubic module that was built in a factory and then assembled on site. Putting the cubes together was like fitting together Lego blocks.

## Sharon Temple

The Sharon Temple, north of Toronto, Canada, was modelled after King Solomon's temple from the Old Testament. It is built from three cubes set on top of each other like three tiers of a wedding cake. The square walls represent the four Gospels and the four directions of north, south, east and west.

# Cubic bubbles

All bubbles are perfect spheres, right? Not when you start with a cubic bubble frame. Here's how.

**You'll need:**

wire that's thin enough to bend and thick enough
   to hold its shape
wire cutters
a piece of corrugated cardboard (the kind used
   for grocery cartons)
scissors
a ruler
a pencil
a compass
a glass jar
bubble mixture

1. Draw a square with sides of 4 cm (1 1/2 inches) on the piece of cardboard and cut it out. You'll use this square as a pattern to make the faces of the wire cube.

2. Cut a length of wire about 90 cm (35 inches) long. Start by forming a 10-cm (4-inch) double loop to be a handle. Twist the wire end around a few times to secure it.

3. Let the wire extend straight about 3 cm (1 inch) past the join of the handle. Give the wire a 90° turn to the right.

4. Use the cardboard square as a guide to bend the wire to make the bottom face of the cube. When you reach the vertex that completes the square, twist the wire around.

5. Next make a vertical face in the same way, using the cardboard square to measure the length of the sides. You'll find that, for some edges, you end up with two strands of wire. Twist the two strands around each other so that the edge is as neat as possible.

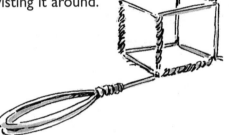

6. Complete the six faces of the cube. Cut off any extra wire and secure the end by twisting it around.

7. Pinch the corners to make the frame as close to a cube shape as you can. (If it isn't perfect, it will still work.)

8. Put some bubble mixture into a glass jar.

You can make some bubble mixture by gently adding 30 mL (2 tbsp.) of dishwashing detergent to 250 mL (1 cup) of lukewarm water. Try not to make a lot of suds.

9. Dip the cubical frame into the jar of bubble mixture, pull it out and prepare for a surprise. You probably have a square in the middle. When you put the frame back in the bubble mix, try to trap an air bubble inside the bubble frame. This time you should have a small cube right at the centre of the bubble frame. Experiment to see the sizes of cubic bubbles you can make with your cubical frame.

### What's happening?

Soap films always contract to form what mathematicians call a "minimal surface." Normally when you blow bubbles, the minimal surface is a sphere. But when the soap film forms on a cubical frame, the minimal surface turns out to be this terrific shape with a square or cube in the centre.

### What happens if . . .
• you blow gently on the cubic bubble at the centre of the bubble frame?
• you blow harder and the bubble floats free of the frame? What shape do you get?

# Answers

## Squaring off, page 12:

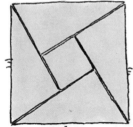

## Square numbers, page 14:

When you subtract each square number from the next one in the series, you get: 1, 3, 5, 7, 9, 11, 13, 15, 17, 19 — all odd numbers! So each square number in the series is the sum of successive odd numbers:

$1 + 3 = 4$
$1 + 3 + 5 = 9$
$1 + 3 + 5 + 7 = 16$
$1 + 3 + 5 + 7 + 9 = 25$

## Which is bigger? page 16:

1. Both pieces of cake are the same size. You can see why when you give the inner square a quarter turn. This means that the square outside the circle has twice the area as the square inside the circle.

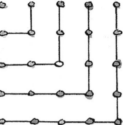

2. The diagonals of the square and the double axe are exactly the same length.

## How many squares? page 18:

There are 30 different squares — 16 squares of 1 square unit; 9 squares of 4 units; 4 squares of 9 units; and don't forget the original square that you started with. (Yep, there are those square numbers again: 16 + 9 + 4 + 1.)

## What's my shape? page 19:
The shape you get is a square.

## Square dissection, page 20:

## Square takeaway, page 21:

## Square Mazes, page 30:

In the church maze, the path to the centre is long and winding, but you eventually get there because there are few branches and blind alleys. The garden maze is trickier.

**Printing with squares, page 34:**

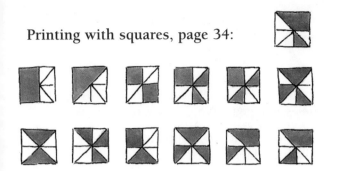

**Tangram, page 41:**

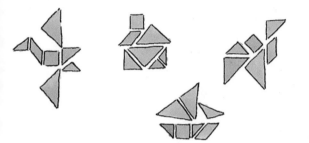

**Polyominoes, page 42:**
These are the five different tetrominoes.

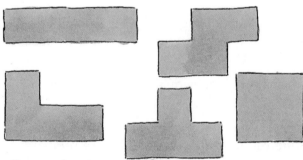

**Pentominoes, page 43:**
This is just one of the possible answers — there are 2338 other solutions to the rectangle puzzle alone.

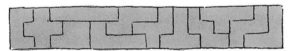

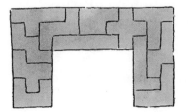
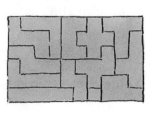

**Cube cuts, page 49:**
The 1-cm (1-inch) cube at the centre of the bigger cube has six faces, each of which requires a separate cut. So it will take at least six cuts to get the 27 small cubes.

**Cross-sections of the cube, page 49:**
Slice the cube like this to get these shapes.

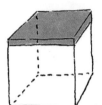      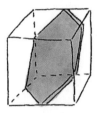

a square              a hexagon

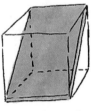      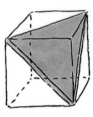

a rectangle            a triangle

**Colouring a cube, page 49:**
You would need three colours. Since the three faces meeting at a corner need to be different, you can't do it in fewer than three colours. And if you make each of the three pairs of opposite faces the same colour, then no adjacent faces are the same.

**Rotating a cube, page 49:**
When you rotate a cube, you get a shape like this:

**Prisms, page 52:**
The least number of straws needed to make the cube stand up is six.

# Glossary

**Angle**  the V-shape formed by two straight lines that intersect at a common point

**Antiprism**  a polyhedron with two identical, parallel faces, whose other faces are all triangles

**Area**  the amount of space inside a closed, flat shape

**Base**  the base is usually taken as the lowest side of a polygon or the lowest face of a polyhedron

**Bisect**  to divide into two equal parts

**Circle**  a closed curve drawn so that every point on the curve is the same distance from a fixed point called the centre

**Degree**  a unit used to measure angles, indicated by the symbol °

**Diagonal**  a line segment, inside a polygon, that joins two vertices

**Edge**  a line segment formed where two faces of a solid meet

**Equilateral triangle**  a triangle with three sides that are the same length

**Face**  any flat side that makes up a solid figure. In a cube, each of the six square sides is a face.

**Hexagon**  a polygon with six sides

**Intersect**  to share at least one point in common. For example, two straight lines can intersect at a common point.

**Midpoint**  the point that divides a line into two equal parts

**Parallel lines**  two lines that are always an equal distance apart

**Parallelogram**  a four-sided polygon having opposite sides parallel

**Polygon**  a closed, flat shape made of straight lines such as a triangle, square or hexagon

**Polyhedron**  a closed, solid shape having polygonal faces, such as a cube

**Prism**  a polyhedron with two indentical, parallel faces, whose other faces are all parallelograms

**Quadrilateral**  a four-sided polygon

**Rectangle**  a parallelogram with four right angles. A square is a special case of a rectangle.

**Regular polygon**  a polygon having all sides the same length and all interior angles the same size

**Right angle**  an angle of 90°, such as this book's corner

**Rhombus**  a parallelogram having four sides that are the same length. A square is a special case of a rhombus.

**Solid**  a three-dimensional figure, such as a cube or sphere

**Symmetry**  repetition of exactly alike parts either on opposite sides of a line or rotated around a central point

**Translation**  a motion where each point on a figure moves sideways, or slides, the same distance and the same direction

**Triangle**  a closed, flat shape with three straight sides

**Vertex**  a point where two sides of a square meet or three edges of a cube meet. The plural is vertices.

**Vertical**  straight up and down

**Volume**  the amount of space inside a solid

# Index